Bangin' The Making of a Y.G. Comprehension & Self Reflective Workbook

Jonas Royster

Bangin' The Making of a Y.G. Comprehension and Self-Reflective Workbook by Jonas Royster

Published by Paradise Publishing Company

www.paradisepublishingcompany.com

ISBN: 978-0-578-89034-0

Printed in United States of America

First Edition

Jonas Royster

30450 Haun Rd. #1041

Menifee, CA

92584

paradisepublishingcompany@gmail.com

Bangin' The Making of a Y.G. is a representation of the Southern California gang culture specifically in San Diego and how a young person's life can switch 180 degrees because of the realities of the American class system. However, even though Deshaun may have felt that there was no other choice but to bang in his new environment he was wrong, there is always a choice. What we choose to do, be, or have is always up to us. The caveat to this is we must come to grips with the consequences of our choices and not point the finger at the circumstances which cause the choice.

Some may say Deshaun was a victim of his circumstances which can be a valid argument but remember P-Nutt gave Deshaun the option to choose, "is you ready to bang little nigga?" was the question. At that moment there was a choice made and the outcome of Deshaun's life was an effect of that choice.

Bangin' could be strictly read for entertainment purposes however it also gives the reader an opportunity to have an experiential lesson if chosen. These question prompts in the workbook are not only about Bangin' The Making of a Y.G. and its story but also about you, the reader. This is a self-reflective learning workbook where it challenges you to take time to reflect on your life, your morals, and your values through the story.

CONTENTS

Bangin' Chapter 1 - 4 7

Bangin' Chapter 5 - 8 10

Bangin' Chapter 9 - 13 13

Bangin' Chapter 14 - 18 17

Bangin' Chapter 19 - 22 21

Bangin' Chapter 23 - 27 25

Bangin' Chapter 28 - 32 28

Bangin' Chapter 33 - 38 31

Bangin' Chapter 39 - 43 35

Bangin' Chapter 44 - 48. 38

Bangin' Chapter 49 - 55. 41

Creating the New You 45

Identifying Routines: How to Dismantle and Create New Ones 50

Personal Responsibility 54

The Magic of Transferable Values 58

Bangin' The Making of a Y.G.
Chapters 1 – 4

1. What were some of the emotions Deshaun might have felt as he and his family moved across town and left his comfort zone?

2. Was Deshaun right or wrong for not stepping in to help Buster Rob? Why?

3. Have you ever been in Deshaun's shoes, where you wanted to do the opposite of what everyone else was doing but for some reason, you didn't listen to your intuition, and you went along with the crowd?

4. How did that turn out for you?

5. What was Deshaun's first "street test"?

6. What was Deshaun's loyalty to Pernell based on?

7. Do you have any similar loyalties?

8. What are some characteristics of Deshaun?

9. What are some characteristics of Pernell?

10. What are your thoughts on Deshaun and Pernell's relationship?

11. Who are you more like Deshaun or Pernell?

12. Your thoughts on the first four chapters?

Bangin' The Making of a Y.G.
Chapters 5 – 8

1. Where did Deshaun and Pernell run to after the fight with the ese's?

2. What gave away that boxing was Pernell's, first love?

3. What are some principles in boxing that can be transferable to gang banging?

4. Why was Deshaun's mom concerned about who he was hanging out with?

5. Who in your life gave you a warning about someone or something that you wish you would have listened to?

6. What was that warning about?

7. What lesson did Deshaun learn from Pernell as they walked to Krystal's house?

8. What are some of the emotions Deshaun might have felt as he watched Pernell run across the street at the driver in the Monte Carlo?

9. Who is B Braze and what are some of his characteristics?

10. Why does B Braze hate Pernell the way he does?

11. Have you hated someone that others thought you should love?

12. How would you describe B Braze's mentality?

13. What are some principles of B Braze?

14. What are your thoughts about the new character B Braze?

Bangin' The Making of a Y.G.
Chapters 9 – 13

1. Who is Tiny Blue Rocc?

2. Why did the author introduce another character with a different point of view?

3. Tiny Blue Rocc mentioned that whenever someone gets out of jail the first thing they eat is Taco Shop. What is going to be your first meal?

4. What is some things Deshaun wrote about in his journal on day 28?

5. In Chapter 11, what is Deshaun contemplating at the end of his journal entry?

6. When was there a time you had to contemplate a decision on either being all in or out?

7. How did it turn out for you?

8. What is the one thing Deshaun said he learned in chapter 12 that if not followed could be a matter of life and death?

9. Being a new booty Deshaun was told by Pernell to guard what with his life and why?

10. What does reputation mean to you?

11. What are the differences between a good reputation and a bad reputation?

12. If we were to ask others about your reputation, what would they say?

13. How has Deshaun's mentality progressed since he moved to the new neighborhood and started hanging out with Pernell?

14. Why do you think Deshaun said yes to the question "are you ready to bang?"

15. What were the 5 p's that Red stated to the crowd after Deshaun got jumped in?

16. What was the second rule that the P-Nutt made clear to everyone that was there?

17. What are some rules that you live by?

Bangin' The Making of a Y.G.
Chapters 14 – 18

1. B Braze left for Arizona after the murder of Lil Blue Rocc but decided to come back to San Diego because it was his "sister's" birthday. When was a time you disregarded your own safety or freedom to remain loyal to someone or something?

2. How has that decision affected your life?

3. What are your thoughts on B Braze so far?

4. Is B Braze wrong for wanting to kill his relative Pernell? Why or why not?

5. What does loyalty mean to you?

6. What are some principles that you are willing to stake your life on?

7. Who was Ms. Jackson to Tiny Blue Rocc?

8. What happened to Tiny Blue Rocc's mother?

9. Do you agree or disagree about Ms. Jackson's comment that "none of this shit is worth it in the end"? Why or why not?

10. What are some things in your life worth dying for (if you have any)?

11. Is there anything worth coming back to jail for?

12. Where did Lil Blue Rocc and Tiny Blue Rocc first meet?

13. According to Tiny Blue Rocc where would he have ended up if it wasn't for meeting Lil Blue Rocc?

14. Who in your life do you give credit to that has given you the "game" to survive in this world?

15. What is the one lesson, saying, rule, or motto that was given to you, that you still live by to this day?

16. How is that lesson productive or counterproductive moving forward in your life?

17. What are your thoughts on Detective Braveheart?

Bangin' The Making of a Y.G.
Chapters 19 – 22

1. What was happening when Deshaun heard what sounded like fireworks?

2. Why did Fly want to wait until their big homies left before they put together a plan?

3. What happened to Pernell's dad?

4. Why does B Braze hate his relative Pernell?

5. What was the first rule Arm & Hammer spoke of before they put together a plan to retaliate?

6. How can that rule be applied to your life now and moving forward?

7. Why do you think Deshaun listened to Arm & Hammer and did not walk away from the huddle like some of their other homies did?

8. What do you think was running across Deshaun's mind as he and Boguard drove to Darlene's house to retaliate?

9. When was there a time in your life when you wish you would have backed out of doing something you knew you had no business doing?

10. What are your thoughts on Deshaun shooting at Darlene?

11. In Deshaun's journal entry on day 44, he mentioned he wanted to talk to somebody about what happened a week earlier but there was no one to talk to. When in your life have you felt the same way?

12. Do you ever wish there was someone you could talk with about life without judgment or consequences?

13. How can Deshaun's mom be so naive to Deshaun's paranoia?

Bangin' The Making of a Y.G.
Chapters 23 – 27

1. How do you feel about Pernell's reason for not wanting Krystal to have his child?

2. Why do you think Deshaun is following Pernell's lead and saying that he's "all in too"?

3. What does "all-in" mean to you?

4. Who is Tiny Blue Rocc to Deshaun?

5. Why is Tiny Blue Rocc disappointed at Deshaun's new affiliation?

6. Have you ever disappointed someone in your life? If so who and why?

7. Why does Deshaun run to the "chaos" and not from it?

8. In Chapter 26 Tiny Blue Rocc finally got his revenge for Lil Blue Rocc's murder. Why do you think retaliation in humans is heavily pursed when harm is done to them or someone close?

9. Deshaun mentioned in chapter 27 that his father would always say after their Saturday morning film sessions "you're only as good as your last play." What does Deshaun's father mean by that?

10. In what areas of your life does the saying "you're only as good as your last play" rear its head in your life?

Bangin' The Making of a Y.G.
Chapters 28 – 32

1. How would you describe Detective Braveheart's character?

2. Detective Braveheart could care less about the two individuals getting jumped in front of the liquor store because he had his own agenda. When have you turned a blind eye towards misbehavior for your own beneficial gain?

3. Why didn't Deshaun tell his side of what happened to him and Sky when Detective Braveheart told him "Look kid, you're the victim. You're not in any trouble, just give me your side of how it all went down."?

4. What are your thoughts on Deshaun and Sky lying to the police so that they wouldn't snitch on his enemies?

5. Deshaun standing up for himself towards Arm & Hammer was critical for the new him (D- Hogg) to emerge and grow. Why do you think people have to become someone new or different to do something they've never done before?

6. When have you ever had to change your identity to fit a new environment?

7. Even though Deshaun seems to have a liking for Sky why didn't Deshaun confirm Sky's hunch?

8. Deshaun is officially "all in" now with the murder of Tiny Awol. Was there a moment in your life that solidify that you were "all in"?

Bangin' The Making of a Y.G.
Chapters 32 – 38

1. Tiny Blue Rocc got all the information he needed from Vanessa so her use for him was done but how do you feel about his statement "Little does she know that it's going to be the last time any of them bitches turn up in life again?"

2. Detective Bravehearts' girlfriend Jenny chose her career over her relationship. When have you chosen something over the people or person you love?

3. Detective Bravehearts C.I. is going against an oath he took with his friends to benefit his own means. What are your thoughts on loyalty?

4. When have you chosen money over moral decision?

5. In chapter 35 Deshaun is writing in his journal reflecting on how much he has learned since moving to the new neighborhood and how the choices he has made were eating at his sanity. Have you ever felt like Deshaun before?

6. When do you take time to reflect on decisions you've made in your life?

7. Describe a time when people close to you gave you advice to not do something however you did it anyway?

8. What was the last advice you gave someone, and they did the complete opposite?

9. Deshaun lost two people close to him in one night. How do you think Deshaun felt knowing he was the catalyst to that event?

10. Like Sky slipping through Deshaun's hands when was there an opportunity that you let slip through your hands that you regret?

11. Deshaun, Pernell, Arm, and Hammer are getting ready to retaliate against who they think killed Boguard and Sky. What does retaliation solve?

12. Why do you think Pernell's choice of retaliating for his homies death over his unborn son makes sense to him?

Bangin' The Making of a Y.G.
Chapters 39 – 43

1. Deshaun and Tiny Blue Rocc were good friends in the past however the lines have been drawn. When have you ever had to draw a hard line on someone you knew or on something in your life?

2. Why has Tiny Blue Rocc decided to murder Deshaun?

3. Should Tiny Blue Rocc murder Deshaun?

4. Throughout the progression of the book, Deshaun is getting bolder and bolder, in your opinion what is happening to Deshaun?

5. Deshaun wants to keep looking for someone to murder after Pernell and Arm & Hammer murder the individual leaving the liquor store. Why do you think Deshaun's not satisfied with that outcome?

6. How hard do you think it was for Deshaun to shoot his old best friend Tiny Blue Rocc?

7. Explain a time you had to choose between two friends or two family members.

8. Deshaun is now the instigator of the violence because of the pain caused to him while at the bonfire. I've once heard the phrase "hurt people hurt people" please explain what that phrase means to you.

Bangin' The Making of a Y.G.
Chapters 44 – 48

1. After being caught with blood on his clothes by his parents Deshaun blames his father for what has transpired. Explain why you think that's a fair statement or not.

2. Why do you think DeShaun's dad is taking a chance to help his son?

3. Auntie Jaleen feels indebted to her brother for what he did in their earlier years. Who or what do you feel indebted to?

4. Why do you think Deshaun's father never told him about going to jail and being charged with murder?

5. Detective Braveheart and Whitehead bent rules to get confessions and evidence they needed to obtain a warrant. What are your thoughts about bending or breaking rules to get what you want?

6. Deshaun's decisions have been based on some of the core values he's adopted during the summer with one of them being loyalty. What is loyalty and where is Deshaun displaying it in chapter 48?

Bangin' The Making of a Y.G.
Chapters 49 – 55

1. Deshaun learned many intangible rules from Pernell that kept him safe in the streets. What are some rules, lessons, or principles that you've been taught that you still live by?

2. In chapter 50 Detective Braveheart stated that "to play the game out here there are no rules, and that's the only rule." From your answers above, which rule is the only rule for you and why?

3. While following Pernell, Deshaun mentioned, "always be committed to your commitments." What are some commitments in your life you wish you would have remained committed to?

4. Why do you believe Deshaun was willing to kill his best friend and in the same situation what would you do?

5. Pernell was willing to sacrifice his life so his unborn son could break the cycle, what sacrifices are you willing to make in your life to break the cycle?

6. What are your thoughts about Pernell's sacrifice?

7. Throughout the book, Detective Braveheart operated outside the law and to the beat of his own drum. How does that make you feel?

8. How do you think it makes others feel when you operate to the beat of your drum?

9. Deshaun mentioned that what Pernell did for Krystal and his unborn seed was real love. What is real love to you?

10. Is Deshaun's mother right, did Pernell force Deshaun into the "life"? What are your thoughts?

11. Deshaun's life changed drastically in four months when he made the decision to bang. Moving forward with your life what decisions are you willing to make that can drastically set your next 12 months up differently?

Creating the New You

To survive and thrive in his new environment, Deshaun had to think like, act like and become a new person. Once he identified those characteristics Deshaun became D-Hogg.

That new self-image was what allowed him to get his first "k" on Tiny Awol, it also permitted him to retaliate when Boguard and Sky were murdered at the bonfire. It also held true in his commitment to murdering his best friend because he believed he broke the number rule. Never snitch.

Deshaun would have never done any of those things mentioned above because of the self-image he held of himself in the years before he moved to his new neighborhood. Deshaun stated in chapter 24 that during the summers he, Lee, and Alex would go to the library and study so they could prepare for college. A person believing they are heading to college will most likely not decide to kill anyone because they hold a high value on life and their future.

One of the best ways to create a new self-image is to identify restrictive beliefs, negative self-statements, and bad habits that no longer serve us. The next step is to create opposing beliefs, statements, and habits that contradict the latter. The most reliable ways to create new self-beliefs are through intentional interruption and constant repetition. This will nurture positive thinking habits and help create a new feedback loop. That is the true sense of leveling up. Great musicians change their self-image all the time. Let's take hip hop for example.

The rapper Lil Wayne has embodied three different personas throughout his career, Weezy, Lil Wayne, and Tunechi as he leveled up. If we closely look at them all three have similar traits however each persona was created to fit a new chapter in his life. Weezy was hungry, flashy, and moved with bravado. Lil Wayne was obsessed with being the best, becoming a killer wordsmith, and he embodied a gang member's personality so he could bully his way through an industry that typically pushed back against down south rappers. Now Tunechi's characteristics are free and easy, fulfilled, lackadaisical, carefree, loving, and content.

Who are you right now? Who do you want to become? The exercise below is designed for you to identify who you are right now so that you can create the person you want to become.
It's called Comfortable Me vs Uncomfortable Me. Who are you today versus who you will be in 12 months.

Realness Alert

This only works if you are 100% honest with yourself. Any fluff will distort your results. List everything you can think of and when you think that's enough come back a day later and write some more. Let's quit lying to ourselves and face the person staring back at us in the mirror. That person is owed more than we are giving to them and it's time to fight for our future selves.

Step 1. Write the name you have been referred to the most in the past 5 to 10 years next to the word Comfortable Me, i.e., when I first did this exercise most people throughout my day referred to me as So Kold, so I wrote So Kold.

Step 2. Next to Uncomfortable Me write the new name you will be referred to and ultimately become, i.e., Jonas Ulysses Royster.

Comfortable Me - So Kold | Uncomfortable Me - Jonas Ulysses Royster

Step 3. Write down the restrictive beliefs, negative self-statements, and bad habits you have today underneath the Comfortable Me.

Comfortable Me - So Kold	Uncomfortable Me - Jonas Ulysses Royster
I'm an alcoholic and a druggie	
I have to hustle because I'm a felon	
I got 99 problems	
I'm cursed	
I'm a professional procrastinator	
I'm never lucky	
Life's a bit** then you die	
I keep getting locked up	
I am So Kold	

Step 4. Underneath Uncomfortable Me, write an opposing belief, statement, or good habit that correlates and counters what you've written underneath Comfortable Me.

Comfortable Me - So Kold	Uncomfortable Me - Jonas Ulysses Royster
I'm an alcoholic and a druggie	I am sober from now on
I have to hustle because I'm a felon	I create my own lane because I am a hustler
I got 99 problems	I have 99 opportunities
I'm cursed	I have the Midas touch
I'm a professional procrastinator	I am a professional action taker
I'm never lucky	Preparation + Opportunity = Luck
Life's a bit** then you die	Life a blessing when you live
I keep getting locked up	I am a square
I am So Kold	I am Jonas Ulysses Royster

Step 5. Do the work, every day. Now that you have your new identity with your new attributes begin to refer to yourself as the new name you wrote next to Uncomfortable Me. Next, find a time in your day that you can read these statements every day to yourself out loud. By reading these new statements you wrote you will begin to rewire your mind. Remember repetition is the mother of habit and the father to change.

Success Cheat Code
Remember any change begins with the belief that if you do the thing long enough you will get the result you're looking for. So if you have been saying, doing, and thinking your Comfortable Me things for over a decade don't expect things to drastically change overnight. If you've walked 50 miles into a forest it will take you 50 miles to walk back out. Be patient with yourself, do the work daily, and eventually you will be the me you wish to be.

Comfortable Me -	Uncomfortable Me -

Identifying Routines: How to Dismantle and Create New Ones

We are all creatures of routine. Some good, some bad, some ugly, and Deshaun was no different. Sometimes we intentionally create them for ourselves and other times we go along with others that are already built out. Sometimes the ones we create are bad and sometimes the ones others create for us are good and sometimes because of the environment, we develop an ugly routine to survive.

Throughout the book, we're able to see different routines that helped and hindered Deshaun for long-term success. We must remember that all routines serve a purpose to obtain a goal however some are for immediate gratification with long-term complications while others forgo the moment at hand for future success. Deshaun had multiple routines throughout the book. In chapter 1 we heard Deshaun speak of the routine that his dad implemented with him when they still lived in Point Loma.

The Routine: Waking up at 9 am every Saturday morning. Watching and breaking down film of his varsity football game from the night before.

The Goal: To become a collegiate athlete.

The Motive: To be like his dad.

This routine can be categorized as good because Deshaun sacrificed immediate gratification (ie. sleep) in hopes of the long-term success of being a collegiate athlete. Now let's look at another routine of Deshaun's once he became D-Hogg.

The Routine: Have a meeting with his homies after any altercations or drama in the streets.

The Goal: To plan out a course of action to retaliate.

The Motive: Not to appear weak to their enemies.

This routine we can categorize as one of those ugly ones because the purpose of the goal was for immediate gratification (i.e., wanting another to feel the same pain) with long-term complications (i.e. death or imprisonment forever).

Now is the time for you to start identifying some of the routines in your life and began to categorize them. Some of these routines we've been doing for so long that we thought this is just how we are however we can change all our routines once we understand what to look for. Here is how to create a new routine.

Step 1. Identify the goal and write it down. (i.e., to be a free man, be sober, stack $10k in a year, get in a healthy and dope ass relationship, start a business.)

Step 2. Find your motive. Why do you want this goal? What makes having this routine so important in your life? What success or happiness will this routine bring into your life?

Step 3. Decide what steps need to be taken. For your routine to be effective and efficient make sure that there are no more than 3 steps. Simplicity beats procrastination and puts you on the fast track to execution.

Step 4. Lay out the plan. Write it down or make a note of it on your phone. Taking that extra step especially when we've never done it before tells the brain that we are committed to doing something new. Remember the brain likes new. If you doubt that ask yourself how you feel when you get a new pair of shoes.

Step 5. Be consistent with your routine. What you practice at you get better with. Remember don't cheat yourself treat yourself. If you need to read the routine before you do it, do that until it becomes automatic.

Simple Life Example

Remember a routine can be made for anything we want to accomplish. I have a morning routine of brushing my teeth as most of us do. My routine consists of brushing each section of my teeth from bottom to top in the order of right, center, and left for 5 seconds twice on each section. My goal is to make sure my breath smells fresh in the morning. My motive, I don't want people to talk about me and say my breath is funky.

Personal Responsibility

Throughout Bangin' The Making of a Y.G. we saw responsibility taken by some characters and shoved away by others. We also saw characters who owned up and took responsibility at certain moments in the story would also deflect responsibility later. No one is perfect especially when it comes to taking responsibility however if we come to an agreement on what defines responsibility then I believe we can take complete ownership of our lives moving forward.

Responsibility is the ability to understand that I am the cause to every effect in my life. Often times we don't want to take ownership of responsibility, so we point our finger to blame someone, something, or some circumstance so we don't have to fix the problem.

Try this exercise, extended your right arm, and point at anything around you. Now look down at your finger that's pointing. Tucked underneath your thumb are three other fingers pointing back at you. Remember we are more responsible for these situations than we think.

Here are 3 benefits you can gain from increasing your personal responsibility:

1. **Power:** You will begin to regain power over the outcomes and circumstances in your lives because you can harness your actions by taking responsibility for your choices. When you blame others, you run away from your responsibility.

2. **Respect:** The more respect you give yourself the more you earn from others. However, to obtain respect is by honoring your word with yourself first. Once you stop disrespecting yourself, it's a trip to see how the world stops disrespecting you as well.

3. **Success:** Success is nothing more than a few simple disciplines applied every day. We must trust the journey and not rush the journey. The Success is the daily work needed to achieve that goal, not the goal itself. The completion of the goal is the byproduct of the work you put in.

So, the question is how do we increase our personal responsibility so that we can regain control of our lives? Here are 5 steps to help build your personal responsibility:

1. **Set clear goals for yourself:** Identify what you want to achieve and create a plan to reach those goals.

2. **Take extreme ownership over your actions:** Acknowledge the impact of your actions and take full responsibility for the outcomes both positive and negative. Remember I am the cause of every effect in my life.

3. **Be accountable**: Hold yourself to a higher standard than others and get it done. Keep a log of your progress when you are accountable to yourself and others.

4. **Communicate effectively:** Develop strong communication skills to express yourself clearly and effectively.

5. **Continuously improve**: Reflection turns experiences into insight so learn from them and make adjustments to your actions and plans as necessary. Continuously strive to improve and grow as a person.

Realness Alert

You will only get back from life what you put into life. So, if you put a little bit in you will only get a little bit back out. And remember you have no one to blame but yourself. You are the cause of every effect in your life. To blame THEM is to ask THEM to fix YOUR problem and THEY don't owe YOU a damn thing!

The Magic of Transferable Values

We've all heard the quote if you stand for nothing you will fall for anything. The real question is, what are you standing on? Living a life as a gang member is a high-risk and stressful life however in order to get through it and escape with your life, your sanity, and respect from others you have to live by a set of values that produce your character. Throughout Bangin' we witnessed each character have a set of core values that they stood on hence making them the person they were.

B Braze, who was an interesting character, had multiple core values from determination to toughness however the one that shined most was his core value of commitment. He was committed to his commitment of killing his own blood relative Pernell. B Braze even admitted that he attempted once before. That is commitment.

Now let's look at Tiny Blue Rocc. Throughout the story all Tiny Blue Rocc wanted was to get his get back for the people who killed his homies. It started with Lil Blue Rocc being killed then later after Deshaun murdered Tiny Awol he wanted revenge for that and got it. That there is the value of integrity. Integrity is doing what you said you were going to do even when no one other than yourself is holding you accountable. As easy as that may sound not a lot of people have the integrity to hold themselves accountable when no one is looking.

Now, what about Deshaun? Deshaun like the other two had more than one core value however the one displayed the most throughout the book was his core value of loyalty. His loyalty was blind and whatever was in the best interest of the set he followed those guidelines regardless of what the outcome was going to be. He was loyal to being loyal to the rules and guidelines. So much so that in the final chapters of the book he was willing to blow his best friend's noodles out of his head because he thought he didn't follow the number one rule. Never snitch.

Most people who have never been in this life or who have never been close to this lifestyle will never understand these values in this context and that is perfectly ok. However, the values that these characters displayed can all be transferred to other areas of life. Even in the sense of the book these values in this context helped them survive however when we transfer them as we began to change our lives these values will allow us to thrive. They will help us grow, succeed, change, garner different skills, and these transferable values become the ladder to get us out of the hole that we dug ourselves into.

However, in order to start the climb up the ladder I suggest you ask yourself that first question. What are my values?

Before I wrote this book and I asked myself that same question. I was living this life for 20 years and I believed I couldn't change because I just didn't know how. I kept asking myself what do I have to offer to society, to my kids, to my wife, to my moms and pops, to my brother, to the workplace, to everything around me.

Truth be told I felt hopeless. I was sick and tired of being sick and tired and I wanted to change. So I looked back at my career in the streets. The only thing I could hang my hat on was my values. Commitment, loyalty, integrity, and discipline.

I harnessed each one of those four core values of mine and transferred them into the writing process as I wrote Bangin' and this workbook. There were too many times to count that I wanted to quit however my value of commitment which is doing the thing you said you were going to do long after the mood you said in has left. I also grabbed onto that loyalty value hard. Meaning that I put this book as my personal priority above all else like I did the homies and the turf. If I was willing to die or go to jail forever for the set because of my loyalty, then I need to have that same energy and loyalty in my own life now.

Our Values are the foundation of everything we've ever accomplished or haven't accomplished in our lives. If a value of mine is being safe, then I most likely wouldn't jump out of a plan. Deshaun's value of loyalty showed up everywhere in the story and he never deviated from it. Why? Because we rarely do things, we don't believe are us. Think about the things you have done in your life. You did them mostly because of some values that you stand on and believe in.

Transferable Values are values that have been applied in one area of life that can now be transferred into a different area. Those past experiences are your proof of concept that your values work for you. Now you use that proof as leverage (to use for gain) against the negative thoughts of "I never did this" and "I don't how to do this."

Example: You were released a week ago and you apply for a new job. You get the call and they want to hire you. It pays exactly what you want but the job starts at 5 am. That start time would require you to wake up at 3:30 am.

Negative Thought: "I ain't never waking up at 3:30 am again in my life! They got me f****** up!"

New Thought: "I woke up 3:30 before for some damn powdered eggs and some janky oatmeal for free, I can damn sure wake at 3:30 am for this money?"

Proof of Concept: Breakfast in the county jail was served at 3:30 am and I would get up every day for that.

Leverage Past Experience: If did it in the county jail I damn sure can do it on the streets.

Transferable Value: Commitment and discipline.

Application: When you are taking risks and going after new opportunities and change in your life use this 5-step process so that you can gain the confidence to succeed.

Below is a list of core values that can help you identify yours. Find the four that most fit you and circle them and then use them as you transition into your new successful life.

- Loyalty
- Spirituality
- Humility
- Compassion
- Honesty
- Kindness
- Integrity
- Selflessness
- Determination
- Generosity
- Courage
- Tolerance
- Trustworthiness
- Equanimity
- Appreciation
- Empathy
- Toughness
- Self-Reliance
- Attentiveness
- Commitment
- Discipline
- Reputation
- Authenticity

Realness Alert

Your life moving forward will be based on the choices you make because of the values you identify from your past experiences. Don't take this lightly because this is the secret that will open doors you used to dream about walking through.

9798988727927